WORLD WAR I
Lost Words

DR NICHOLAS SAUNDERS

KEY TO IMPORTANT ARTICLES

Look out for the following symbols through this book, highlighting key articles from the past.

FILM EXCERPT
Primary source material taken from a film about the subject matter.

SONG EXCERPT
Lyrics extracted from songs about the subject matter.

OFFICIAL SPEECH
Transcribed words from official government speeches.

GOVERNMENT DOCUMENT
Text extracted from an official government document..

LETTER
Text taken from a letter written by a participant in the events.

PLAQUE/INSCRIPTION
Text taken from plaques/monuments erected to remember momentous events described in this book.

INTERVIEW/BOOK EXTRACT
Text from an interview/book by somebody there at the time.

NEWSPAPER ARTICLE
Extracts taken from newspapers of the period.

TELEGRAM
Text taken from a telegram sent to or by a participant in the events.

Copyright © ticktock Entertainment Ltd 2005
First published in Great Britain in 2005 by ticktock Media Ltd.,
Unit 2, Orchard Business Centre, North Farm Road, Tunbridge Wells, Kent, TN2 3XF
ISBN 1 86007 831 1 pbk
Printed in China
A CIP catalogue record for this book is available from the British Library.

CONTENTS

INTRODUCTION

T he First World War changed the world, and produced an unbridgeable divide between pre-war civilization and the new harsher existence which followed. The Great War created the modern world in which we live today. Before 1914, the world was dominated by the economic might of Britain and France, and the imperial powers of Europe; royal families that were the focus of loyalty and tradition and had close links with each other.

For several hundred years, the wider world had been shaped and controlled by European nations. Africa, India, the Americas, the Middle East and the Far East had all been conquered and colonised by the British, French, German, Dutch, Spanish, and Portuguese. Sea power was vital in order to maintain these far-off territories. In the nineteenth century, Britain's Royal Navy was very powerful.

Above A map of the Balkans region (top) and (above) a map of the world before the outbreak of war. Britain's colonies are shown in pink.

Below A gas mask and other weapons used in the war. World War 1 was the first time such sophisticated weapons had been used on such a scale.

By the end of the nineteenth century, the world had been shaped by European civilization and its scientific and technological superiority. One of the effects of the First World War was that this technology was used against the

countries that had developed it. It was regarded as the first global or worldwide conflict, but it was also a bitterly destructive European civil war. By its end, Europe's royal families had been swept away, and new nations had emerged. World War I was also known as the Great War, because people believed that war on such a scale would never happen again. But injustices committed during the war caused resentment that eventually led to a second, even more destructive and terrible world war in 1939.

Developments in technology meant killing and wounding on a scale that could not previously have been imagined. Politicians and generals, whose experiences of war had been in far smaller nineteenth century conflicts, were unable to grasp the implications of the new weapons they possessed. The failure to understand these developments led to the vast and tragic numbers of dead and wounded at such battles as the Somme and Verdun in 1916, and Passchendaele in 1917, and to the untold numbers of 'The Missing' whose bodies were never found.

The Great War was also different in the way that it affected civilians at home. Foreigners caught

Above French poster proclaiming the modern aircraft at the country's disposal during the conflict.

Below Archduke Franz Ferdinand (left) walks with Kaiser Wilhelm of Germany.

Left A soldier in the British Royal Naval Division relaxes. The Division fought in many of the major battles in the war, including the Somme.

LA PUISSANCE MILITAIRE DE LA FRANCE

5

Above *Ferdinand and his wife Sophie just moments before the Archduke was assassinated.*

by the outbreak of war, in what had become an enemy country overnight, were incarcerated in internment camps. Across mainland Europe, civilians were forced to become refugees as the war stagnated into four years of trench warfare on the Western and Eastern Fronts.

The conflict also led to rapid technological development, which changed the nature and balance of international relations and military capabilities. When the war began, aviation was in its infancy, and the Wright Brothers' first powered flight had taken place in North Carolina less than eleven years earlier. Aircraft soon became a central feature of modern warfare. Aeroplane technology allowed aerial dogfights between opposing squadrons and aerial bombing raids. It also contributed to rapid development in camera and radio technology used in reconnaissance and communications. Similarly, the pre-war world had been dominated by hugely expensive navies. Between 1914 and 1918, Germany developed U-boat submarines that made

Above *A US badge urging men to join the United States armed forces.*

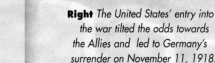

Right *The United States' entry into the war tilted the odds towards the Allies and led to Germany's surrender on November 11, 1918.*

these navies largely obsolete. Explosive shells, machine guns, tanks, and gas were all perfected during World War I, and changed the nature of war permanently.

The First World War also made a deep impression on society and culture. More women entered the workforce and became aware of a new way of life. British women won the right to vote in 1919, and American women in 1920, as a direct result. A whole generation of young British men died, and many more returned shell-shocked or maimed. Directly after the war there was a short period of prosperity. People wanted to have fun after four years of gloom, and it became known as the 'Roaring Twenties'. The fun did not last long, as the collapse of the financial markets in Wall Street in New York in 1929 led to the worldwide Depression of the 1930s. The world was also different politically. The map of Europe had been redrawn, and Germany was resentful because it felt humiliated by the terms of the Peace Treaty of Versailles. This was one of the factors that led to the outbreak of World War II in 1939.

Above *World War 1 left a powerful legacy, including a settlement which led to an almost inevitable second conflict and in turn, the division of the world into East and West. In Europe, Berlin was divided between the Communist East and Capitalist West by a wall which stood until 1989.*

Below *The Battle of Lorette lasted 12 months from October 1914 to October 1915. More than 100,000 people were killed. The cemetery contains more than 20,000 tombs.*

The Great War has remained in the minds of people in Europe and the places that were part of former empires. Today, it is a multi-million pound commercial enterprise involving books, the media and battlefield tours. This may be because of the dramatic way in which it changed people's ideas about the world they lived in, but it is an unexpected legacy of the war that was supposed to end all wars.

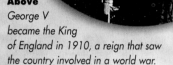

Above
*George V
became the King
of England in 1910, a reign that saw
the country involved in a world war.*

The course and consequences of the First World War are well known, but it is more difficult to understand why it began, and why it involved so many nations. Among its many causes were existing political instability in a part of Europe known as the Balkans, treaties that connected one country with another, nationalism, rivalry between different countries, and the lack of imagination of the politicians, members of royalty and generals, who could not see what a war on such a scale might mean.

"I have frequently been astonished to hear with what composure and how glibly Members, and even Ministers, talk of a European war. [Previously wars had been fought]... 'by small regular armies of professional soldiers'... [but in the future, when]... mighty populations are impelled on each other [such a conflict would end]... in the ruin of the vanquished and the scarcely less fatal commercial dislocation and exhaustion of the conquerors... The wars of peoples will be more terrible than those of kings."

Winston Churchill on May 13, 1901, warned in parliament that future wars would be different from previous ones.

EUROPEAN ROYALTY AND MONEY

The Great War was in many respects a European civil war. It was also a war between different branches of Europe's royal houses. Russia's Czar Nicholas II and Germany's Kaiser Wilhelm II – as well as others – were related, and appeared together in a famous family photograph with the late Queen Victoria. Half-German herself, the queen had married the German Prince Albert of Saxe-Coburg-Gotha.

At the outbreak of war, 28 per cent of Germans studying at Oxford University were members of the German aristocracy. The worlds of finance and business were also linked, and the leading City of London banking families, the Rothschilds and the Kleinworts, were of German origin. These royal and financial connections and self-interest meant that Europe was ruled by different branches of the same extended royal family. It was clear to many that any

Right *A lavish banquet was held at Buckingham Palace for Queen Victoria's Golden Jubilee. All of the crowned heads of state of Europe were invited. Some would be at war with each other a few years later.*

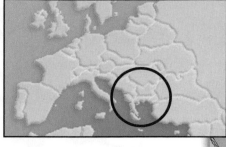

European war would shake these thrones and would be best avoided.

BALKAN TINDERBOX
By 1914, the Balkan region of Eastern Europe was a time-bomb waiting to explode. The most important regional power was the multi-ethnic Austro-Hungarian empire based in Vienna. Its 50 million people were a volatile mix of ethnic groups, each agitating for various degrees of independence and territorial claims. In 1908, the empire annexed Bosnia and Herzegovina – a majority of whose population shared their language and culture with Serbia. When Germany supported Austria-Hungary, Serbian and Russian resistance to the annexation faded. Complicating matters further, Bulgaria, Greece, Montenegro, and Serbia joined forces to win various other territories in the region, but Austria and Italy intervened and an independent Albania was created.

Above *A map showing the Balkan area of Europe. Conflict between the different ethnic groups in the area was a major factor in plunging the world into conflict.*

Left *Baronne de Rothschild, part of the famous banking family living in London, was of German extraction. There were many links between the two countries before war broke out.*

TIMELINE 1900-1912

1900
Germany out-produces British steel production and emerges as a major industrial power and rival to Britain.

MAY 13, 1901
Winston Churchill warns of the unrecognised dangers of a European war.

1906
Britain launches HMS *Dreadnought*, a new class of super battleship.

1908
Austria-Hungary annexes Bosnia and Herzegovina.

1912
First Balkan War, Serbia victorious over Turkey.

"... a European war is bound to come sooner or later, in which the issue will be one of a struggle between Germandom and Slavdom... [and that]... to prepare themselves for that contingency is the duty of all States which are the champions of Germanic ideas and culture."

Helmuth von Moltke, the Chief of the German Imperial General Staff, speaking to General Conrad von Hötzendorf, the Austrian Chief of Staff on February 10, 1913.

Above Built in 1906, the British battleship Dreadnought was the largest ship of its kind in the world.

Above Count Ferdinand von Zeppelin, creator of the first fleet of Zeppelin airships.

casualties during the American Civil War caused by artillery, the sheer scale of Great War bombardments using millions of shells was a terrifying and expensive development. The need to make more and more munitions brought women into the labour force and so involved large numbers of civilians. Other new weapons of mass killing included poisonous gas and machine guns, and there was also the development of aerial bombardment using aeroplanes and German Zeppelins. This was another factor that led to the creation of 'total war' or war that involved whole nations. Air raids were frequently aimed at civilian targets, especially in Britain. The British military developed the world's first tank, and the Germans perfected submarine warfare. This type of technology changed the face of war, and new military thinking was needed to take advantage of it.

Serbia and Bulgaria then fell out and went to war in 1913 – Bulgaria losing territory as a result. By June 1914, the Balkan region was unstable because of nationalism, rivalry between people from different ethnic groups, and political dissent.

THE WEAPONS OF TOTAL WAR

The Great War was the first global industrialised conflict, and its possible consequences were not really understood when hostilities began. Although there had been terrible

THE MOST POWERFUL NAVY IN THE WORLD

Admiral Horatio Nelson won a major victory for Britain against the French at the Battle of Trafalgar in 1805. Since then, Britain's Royal Navy had commanded the world's seas,

"The news continues to be good, the Tanks seem to have done good work and fairly put the wind up the Hun who was seen to run like Hell in front of them shouting "This isn't war, it is murder". for once in the war we come into the field with a new engine of war and not second-hand copied from the Hun."

Major HE Trevor, 37th Infantry Brigade, wrote to his parents from the Somme on September 16, 1916 about the role of tanks. No new weapon captures the essence of industrialised war better than the tank.

Below *The development of aircraft was to lead to a new type of warfare - aerial warfare. Bombs could be dropped from the side and machine guns fired from the cockpit.*

TIMELINE 1913-1914

1913
Second Balkan War; Germany's standing army reaches 544,000 men.

JULY 29, 1914
Czar Nicholas sends telegram to Kaiser Wilhelm asking him to avoid war.

helping to forge and maintain the empire created during the reign of Queen Victoria from 1838 to 1901. Between then and 1914, no other country had dared to oppose Britain's huge and intimidating naval power. Naval technology had changed, and battleships were built of steel, not wood. They were powered by steam rather than sails, and explosive shells had replaced cannonballs. HMS *Dreadnought* launched in 1906 had revolutionised battleship design with its thick armour plating and massive firepower. But these new developments had never been tested in full-scale battle. Between 1898 and 1900, the German Admiral Alfred von Tirpitz formed a plan to build

Above *The submarine came of age during the World War 1. German U-boats sank 325 merchant ships during the war.*

Left *The use of machine guns during the war would dramatically escalate the scale of casualties.*

"In April 1916, Polly, a workmate of mine, and myself decided we would get a job on munitions. After some controversy about my age, I was only seventeen just, and the authorised age was eighteen, I was taken on as an overhead-crane driver… My first impression was sheer fright, rows and rows of 8-inch, 6-inch and 9-inch shells not forgetting the 12-inch which reached to my waist and higher… We were on eight-hour shifts… but this was changed to twelve hours…"

Huge numbers of women took employment in munitions factories thereby freeing the men for the war; 17-year old Lottie Wiggins recalls starting work in the munitions factory.

Above *Archduke Franz Ferdinand (left) was shot dead by the Bosnian Serb Gavrilo Princip.*

Serbia. On July 29, Serbia's ally Russia began to mobilise troops against Austria–Hungary, thus also threatening Germany. On August 1, Germany declared war on Russia. On August 3, it invaded Russia's ally France and its tiny neighbour Luxembourg. On August 4, Germany invaded Belgium.

THE SCHLIEFFEN PLAN

Named after the German military strategist Count Alfred von Schlieffen (1833-1913), this was designed to enable Germany to fight on two fronts. The idea was that Russia's

a High Seas Fleet that could challenge the Royal Navy's mastery of the oceans and thus Britain's empire.

ASSASSINATION IN SARAJEVO

On June 28, 1914, Archduke Ferdinand, the heir to the Austro-Hungarian throne, and a critic of Serbian nationalism, was on a state visit to Sarajevo. Austria–Hungary had made political demands on Serbia which had not been fully met. Ferdinand was assassinated by 18-year old Bosnian Serb student Gavrilo Princip – a member of the Serbian nationalist group 'Black Hand'. On July 28, Austria–Hungary, supported by its ally Germany, declared war on

"She had literally been blown to fragments. The floor, the walls, the ceilings were splotched with - well, it's enough to say that the woman's remains could only have been collected with a shovel."

On August 25, 1914, the German Zeppelin airship dropped bombs on the Belgian port of Antwerp, killing Belgian citizens in their own houses. The American newspaper correspondent E. Alexander Powell wrote on seeing what had happened to a woman killed in her home.

Right *Alfred von Tirpitz introduced the First Fleet Act in 1898, and a Second Fleet Act in 1900. They outlined a principle of building a German Navy to rival that of Britain.*

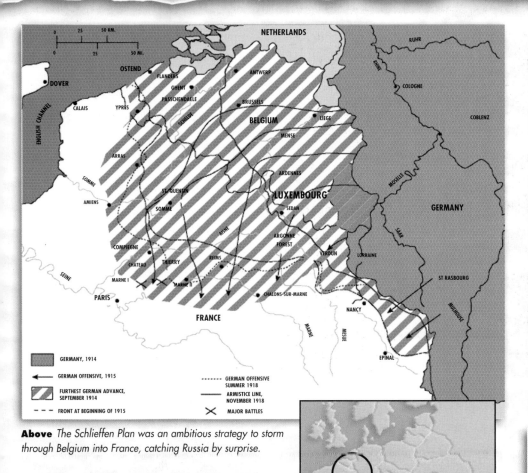

Above The Schlieffen Plan was an ambitious strategy to storm through Belgium into France, catching Russia by surprise.

JUNE 28, 1914
Archduke Ferdinand assassinated in Sarajevo.

JULY 29, 1914
Russia begins mobilization.

AUG 4, 1914
Britain declares war on Germany.

AUG 5-6, 1914
Belgian town of Hervé decimated by German troops in act of reprisal.

Below Helmuth von Moltke took over the running of the Schlieffen Plan after Schlieffen died in 1913.

slow mobilisation would give time for a huge German force to storm through Belgium and thereby outflank the more heavily defended French border further south. Paris would be taken quickly, dealing the French army's morale a lethal blow. Germany would then send reinforcements east to confront the Russians. Schlieffen died in 1913, so his successor Helmuth von Moltke (1848-1916) was left to enact the plan. But Moltke withdrew six western divisions and transferred them east, which fatally reduced the mass and momentum of the attack on France. The German advance was halted at the First Battle of the Marne in September 1914. Arguments still continue as to whether the plan might actually have been unworkable from the start.

"He was worried about the Russian armaments, about the planned railway construction, and detected [in these] the preparations for a war against us in 1916. He complained about the inadequacy of the rail links that we had to the Western Front against France; and hinted... [at] whether or not it would not be better to strike now, rather than to wait."

In June 1914, the banker Max Warburg recalled this conversation with Kaiser Wilhelm. The Kaiser was deeply worried about Germany's ability to move troops between the Eastern and Western fronts efficiently.

Above German troops amass outside Belgium in preparation for invasion.

The German army invaded France, Luxembourg and Belgium at the beginning of August 1914. This broke the terms of the 1839 Treaty of London which guaranteed Belgium's neutrality, so Britain entered the war on August 4. A small British Expeditionary Force (BEF) of 120,000 men began to arrive in France on August 12, and quickly became involved in the Battle of Mons and the subsequent retreat. The German advance was rapid, efficient, and successful, pushing on towards Paris as Schlieffen had planned...

"Happy are they who
die for they return
Into the primeval clay
and the primeval earth
Happy are they who
die in a just war
Happy as the ripe corn
and the harvested grain."

The romantic notions held by many of the first war recruits was captured by the French poet Charles Péguy who wrote a poem which illustrates how neither he nor anyone else understood what was to come.

GERMANY ADVANCES TO THE GATES OF PARIS

Following the Schlieffen Plan, the German Fourth Army moved rapidly to occupy Luxembourg by August 3, and the Second Army crossed the Belgian border the following day. On August 16, after 11 days of German bombardment and siege, the fortified city of Liège capitulated. As Schlieffen had foreseen, the French, under General Joffre, responded by invading Alsace and Lorraine, far to the south-east of the exposed Belgian border. The French strike, Plan XVII, was a failure, and drew valuable troops away from the area that the Germans planned to attack. On August 16, the

Below General von Kluck (with overcoat) and his staff. He was an aggressive commander, a factor that contributed towards the failure of the Schlieffen Plan.

"There was such a rush for fellows to go in the Army they they'd had to get quite a number of officers in to deal with all these recruits... I was only eighteen and I didn't weigh very much - I didn't look very much like a soldier - I weighed 8 stone 11 lb., but I was passed."

Gunner R. Lewis, Royal Garrison Artillery recalls how he was admitted into the Army.

Above *French on the firing line at the First Battle of the Marne.*

German First Army, under Alexander von Kluck, invaded Belgium, took Brussels, then moved south, forcing the French and the BEF, under Field Marshal Lord Haig, to retreat from Charleroi and Mons. By early September, German forces had achieved a string of victories and were less than 30 miles from Paris.

THE BATTLE OF THE MARNE AND GERMAN RETREAT

The German advance had been spectacular but its speed left soldiers exhausted, their uniforms in tatters, and with serious communication and logistical problems. Between September 5 and 10, French and British forces counter–attacked near Paris by the Marne river, at what has become known as the First Battle of the Marne. Armies attacked each other over open fields, and fortunes were mixed. French reinforcements arrived from Paris in taxis, and the French Fifth Army and the BEF advanced into the yawning gap between the German First and Second armies.

TIMELINE
1914

AUG 3, 1914
German soldiers occupy Luxembourg.

AUG 13, 1914
German army invades Belgium.

AUG 24-30, 1914
British retreat from Mons.

SEPT 3, 1914
German cavalry patrols get to within 8 miles of Paris.

5-10 SEPTEMBER, 1914
First battle of the Marne stops German advance and pushes them back east to the Chemin des Dames.

12 OCT-11 NOV, 1914
First Battle of Ypres - neither side gains advantage.

Left *Countryside in the French region of Alsace, eastern France, invaded during the Battle of the Marne.*

"In a side street off the Strand I met a jolly little dachshund - the dachshund might be called the national dog of Germany - walking cheerfully along well-bedecked in red, white and blue ribbons. And around his neck he wore this label, "I am a naturalised British subject". And he seemed mighty proud of the fact, too."

On August 18, 1914, the Daily Mirror in England carried the following article, showing to what bizarre extremes patriotism and anti-German feeling would go.

Above *Lord Kitchener's famous poster aided recruitment into Britain's army in 1914.*

By September 13, the Germans had retreated to the heights of the Chemin des Dames and east to Verdun. The Schlieffen Plan had failed.

THE CHRISTMAS TRUCES OF 1914

Unofficial and spontaneous Christmas truces took place at many sites along the Western Front during December 1914. Military authorities on both sides prohibited them, but German and British soldiers nevertheless met in no man's land, exchanged food and drink and chatted. At 'Plug Street Wood' in Belgium, Captain C I Stockwell of the Royal Welch Fusiliers recalled how his truce ended. At 8.30 am on December 26 he fired three shots in the air and put up a flag saying 'Merry Christmas'. The German Captain responded by putting up a sheet with 'Thank you' written on it. Both men climbed onto their parapets, bowed and saluted each other, and climbed back down into their trenches. The German captain fired two shots in the air and hostilities were resumed.

A NEW KIND OF CONFLICT

By early 1915, it had become clear that this was a new kind of war, of entrenched positions rather than rapid movement, of large civilian armies rather than small professional ones. This was industrialised total war – a new phenomenon in history, that involved civilians as well as soldiers.

Right *An artist's impression of the Christmas Truce in the Trenches, based on a description by a rifleman witness .*

"The whole idea was to get hold of a rifle, learn to shoot a bit, proceed to France at the earliest possible moment, kill vast quantities of Germans, possibly get wounded in some artistic place, win the war and march back with Colours flying and bands playing and the girls falling on your neck."

Several million men responded to Lord Kitchener's call for volunteers in 1914 and 1915, often joining with a totally false idea of what was going to happen. Captain Alan Goring, MC, recalls his expectations upon signing up.

Above Poster remembering the sinking of the luxury passenger ship the Lusitania by a German submarine.

TIMELINE
1914-1915

SEPT, 1914
After only six weeks of war, half a million British men volunteer for Kitchener's army.

SEPT-OCT, 1914
On the Western Front, German and Allied armies grind to a halt and trench warfare begins.

NOV, 1915
Winston Churchill, First Lord of the Admiralty, suggests invading Turkey's Gallipoli peninsula.

DEC, 1914
Unofficial Christmas truces between German and Allied soldiers take place at various places along the Western Front.

MAY 7, 1915
German submarine U-20 sinks the passenger liner Lusitania off the southern Irish coast.

Britain raised a huge volunteer army – Kitchener's Army – and brought women into the munitions factories to free men to fight. The war created appalling conditions of combat, and led to terrible wounds, the trauma of shell shock, and vast numbers of casualties. It also produced a new world of the trench and the dugout, and enduring popular sayings, including 'going over the top' (of a trench, into battle), and 'no man's land' (the no-go area between armies) which are still used today. The war also began to claim civilian casualties when, in May 1915, the unarmed passenger ship Lusitania was sunk by the German submarine U-20. 1198 people were drowned.

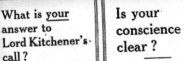

Above An advertisement in an Irish newspaper urging the male population to do the honourable thing and sign up.

LEARNING THE HARD WAY

1915 was a bad year for the Allies. Flawed military tactics showed up the mismatch between 19th-century ideas and 20th-century technology. On the battle line between the Allied and German armies, otherwise known as the Western Front, Allied forces won the

"Enormous noise. Continuous explosion. A deserted landscape... Men were eating, smoking, doing odd jobs but no one was fighting. A few were peering in periscopes or looking through loopholes."

First impressions of life in the front-line trenches often bewildered new recruits. R. Mottram wrote of his first impressions.

> "One of the weapons contemplated was poison gas, in particular chlorine, which was blown towards the enemy from the most advanced positions. When I objected that this was a mode of warfare violating the Hague Convention, he said that the French had already started it…"

German officer Otto Hahn first heard in January 1915 that the Germans were to use poison gas on the battlefield around Ypres, Belgium in order to break the deadlock of the trenches.

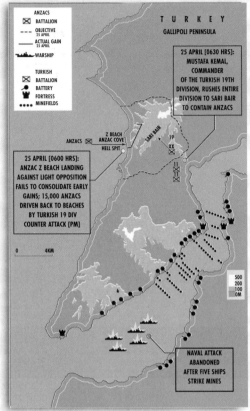

Above *A map showing the fateful Gallipoli invasion.*

Map labels:

ANZACS
⊠ BATTALION
- - - OBJECTIVE 25 APRIL
—— ACTUAL GAIN 25 APRIL
⛴ WARSHIP

TURKISH
⊠ BATTALION
♠ BATTERY
♜ FORTRESS
•••• MINEFIELDS

TURKEY
GALLIPOLI PENINSULA

25 APRIL [0630 HRS]: MUSTAFA KEMAL, COMMANDER OF THE TURKISH 19TH DIVISION, RUSHES ENTIRE DIVISION TO SARI BAIR TO CONTAIN ANZACS

25 APRIL [0600 HRS]: ANZAC Z BEACH LANDING AGAINST LIGHT OPPOSITION FAILS TO CONSOLIDATE EARLY GAINS; 15,000 ANZACS DRIVEN BACK TO BEACHES BY TURKISH 19 DIV COUNTER ATTACK [PM]

Z BEACH
ANZAC COVE
HELL SPIT
SARI BAIR
ANZACS ⊠

0 ___ 4KM

500 200 100 0M

NAVAL ATTACK ABANDONED AFTER FIVE SHIPS STRIKE MINES

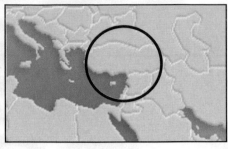

battle of Neuve Chapelle in March, but suffered terrible losses in the Second Battle of Ypres in April and May, when the Germans attacked using poisonous gas. Between May 4 and June 18, the French suffered appalling casualties in the Second Battle of Artois, as did British and Indian troops at Aubers Ridge near Neuve Chapelle. After the Battle of Loos between 25 September and 16 October, almost 16,000 British were dead or missing and 34,580 wounded. No progress had been made. In an

Below *A Naval landing party coming into Kum Kaleh in Gallipoli, Turkey.*

MARCH 10-13, 1915
Battle of Neuve Chapelle,
Allies win control.

APRIL 22-MAY 27, 1915
Second Battle of Ypres.

APRIL 25
Allied troops land at Cape
Helles on the Gallipoli peninsula.

DEC 1915-JAN, 1916
Allied forces evacuate Gallipoli
after 200,000 die.

Above *Australian troops survey the damage during the Gallipoli offensive of 1915.*

attempt to break the deadlock on the Western Front, the British Government decided to open a new front, on the Gallipoli peninsula in Turkey.

GALLIPOLI 1915

Winston Churchill chose to attack Gallipoli in the hope of penetrating the Dardanelles straits and thus knocking Germany's ally out of the war. Allied naval action failed, and several battleships were sunk by mines. A mishandled land invasion on April 25 trapped British, French, and ANZAC (Australian and New Zealand) troops on the beaches. The Turkish troops were commanded by German general Liman von Sanders. One participant who distinguished himself was Mustapha Kemal. He later became Turkey's president under the name Kemal Atatürk. Allied attacks at Cape Helles, Anzac Cove, and Suvla Bay failed. Troops suffered dreadful conditions and appalling casualties. On October 16, Allied commander Sir Ian Hamilton was removed, and Allied troops were evacuated in December. No advantage had been gained, but 200,000 Allied soldiers died.

Right *Mustapha Kemal rose to prominence during the the Gallipoli offensive against the Allies.*

> "We landed on a spit of land which in those days we called Shrapnel Point… There were lines of men clinging like cockroaches under the cliffs… The only thing to be done was to dig in… but a good many men were shot while they were doing this…. As it was, we had to put six hundred men on the ship from which we had embarked in the morning… under the charge of one officer, a veterinary surgeon!"
>
> *Landing on Gallipoli's beaches was a deadly affair, as recorded by Captain The Honourable Aubrey Herbert, a soldier in the Irish Guards, on April 25, 1915.*

CHAPTER 3

THE CRISIS DEEPENS MASS SLAUGHTER

Above Erich von Falkenhayn was criticised for his tactics at Verdun that led to the deaths of tens of thousands of German soldiers.

By the end of 1915 it was obvious to all sides that this was a war in which armies would attack each other from trenches. It was also clear that it would involve huge numbers of men and materiel. Ideas about how the war should be fought, however, did not keep pace with the new technologies of war. During 1916 and 1917, old ideas and new weapons came into conflict at the battles of Verdun, the Somme and the Third Ypres (Passchendaele), leaving behind them terrible, almost unimaginable numbers of dead and wounded. These battles have become the icons of and bywords for the madness and futility of industrialised war.

"At my feet two unlucky creatures rolled the floor in misery. Their clothes and hands, their entire bodies were on fire. They were living torches. (The next day) In front of us on the floor the two I had witnessed ablaze, lay rattling. They were so unrecognisably mutilated that we could not decide on their identities. Their skin was black entirely. One of them died that same night. In a fit of insanity the other hummed a tune from his childhood, talked to his wife and his mother and spoke of his village. Tears were in our eyes"

French soldier Louis Barthas describes witnessing the horrific deaths of two German soldiers.

Above French troops at Douaumont prepare for battle.

Above Kaiser Wilhelm (left) with von Hindenburg and Ludendorff, planning battle lines.

TIMELINE
1916

FEB 21, 1916
Germans launch artillery barrage and attack on Verdun.

FEB 22-29, 1916
Fierce fighting and German capture of Fort Douaumont.

APRIL 20, 1916
French counter-attack repulsed by the German army.

Below A line of crosses for soldiers killed at Verdun.

WHY VERDUN?

The town of Verdun in north-east France, and its ring of protective forts on either side of the River Meuse, had no strategic value either for the Germans or the French. Nevertheless it became the bloodiest battleground of the war. In February 1916, prompted by his policy of attrition, German General Erich von Falkenhayn chose to attack Verdun. He aimed not for a breakthrough but rather to wear down the French Army. French commander General Joseph Joffre was so confident that the forts of Douaumont, Vaux, and Thiaumont could withstand attack that just before the battle he had their defences dismantled and their guns removed.

SACRED BATTLEFIELD

On February 21, 1916, the Germans bombarded the French lines with a million shells, and within a few days Fort Douaumont had fallen. Joffre was immediately replaced by General Pétain, commander of the French

"The losses are registered as follows: they are dead, wounded, missing, nervous wrecks, ill and exhausted. Nearly all suffer from dysentery. Because of the failing provisioning the men are forced to use up their emergency rations of salty meats. They quenched their thirst with water from the shellholes. They have to build their own accommodation and are given a little cacao to stop the diarrhoea. The latrines, wooden beams hanging over open holes, are occupied day and night - the holes are filled with slime and blood."

A German witness writes about the state of his fellow soldiers during the Verdun offensive in 1916.

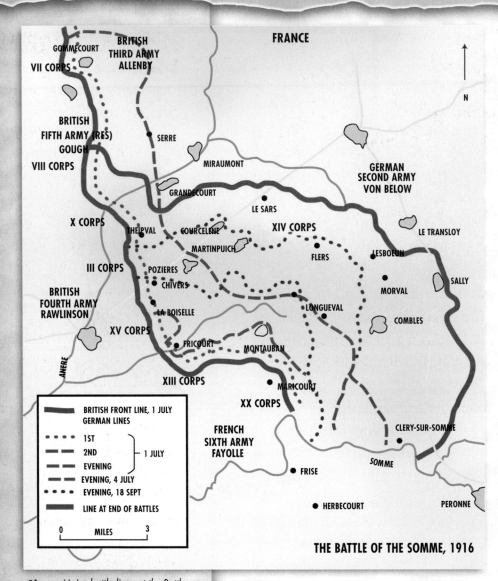

THE BATTLE OF THE SOMME, 1916

Map labels:

FRANCE

GOMMECOURT
BRITISH THIRD ARMY ALLENBY
VII CORPS
BRITISH FIFTH ARMY (RES) GOUGH
SERRE
VIII CORPS
MIRAUMONT
GERMAN SECOND ARMY VON BELOW
GRANDECOURT
LE SARS
X CORPS
THIEPVAL
COURCELENE
XIV CORPS
LE TRANSLOY
MARTINPUICH
FLERS
LESBOEUN
III CORPS
POZIERES
SALLY
CHIVERS
MORVAL
BRITISH FOURTH ARMY RAWLINSON
LA BOISELLE
LONGUEVAL
COMBLES
XV CORPS
FRICOURT
MONTAUBAN
ANCRE
XIII CORPS
MARICOURT
XX CORPS
CLERY-SUR-SOMME
FRENCH SIXTH ARMY FAYOLLE
SOMME
FRISE
HERBECOURT
PERONNE

Legend:

━━━	BRITISH FRONT LINE, 1 JULY
	GERMAN LINES
•••••	1ST ⎤
– – –	2ND ⎬ 1 JULY
— — —	EVENING ⎦
—•—•	EVENING, 4 JULY
•••••	EVENING, 18 SEPT
━━━	LINE AT END OF BATTLES

0 — MILES — 3

Above *Major battle lines at the Battle of the Somme, 1916.*

Second Army. From this point, Verdun became a symbol of France's will to endure and win, and the prospect of defeat or surrender was judged to be a political impossibility. Falkenhayn's hope that his attack would suck in virtually the entire French Army was realised when 259 of the 330 French infantry divisions became embroiled in the carnage. Attack and counter-attack raged from February to November, with artillery, aeroplanes, flamethrowers and gas all used in the desperate struggle. Fort Vaux was overrun by the Germans in June, and Fort Douaumont was retaken by the French in October. No side could win a decisive advantage, and the battle became a deadly grinding machine for both armies. As Christmas approached, it became clear that the French had held on and Verdun was saved.

BATTLE AT THE SOMME

The Somme offensive was planned in December 1915 as a joint British

"10th July /16. Dawn patrol. This is the most impressive time of day to be out. The light has barely come and gun flashes twinkle all over the country in little points of blue flame. From time to time rockets soar up into the grey dawn. Flares glow like fires in the trenches and far over in Hun-land the white plume of a train."

Logbook entry by Cecil Lewis, a pilot in the Royal Flying Corps (RFC) concerning the Battle of the Somme.

Above *Allied soldiers taking part in trench warfare during the Battle of the Somme.*

Above *King George V (centre) with, left to right, Marshal Joffre; General Poincare; General Foch and Field Marshal Lord Haig at Beauquesne, France.*

and French attack designed to wear down the German army's reserve forces. The German attack on Verdun in February 1916 changed things dramatically. French soldiers were drawn away from the Somme to reinforce Verdun, leaving the bulk of the attack to the British Fourth Army, commanded by Sir Henry Rawlinson. The disastrous outcome was partly due to the fact that there were two different battle plans. Rawlinson favoured a 'bite-and-hold' operation involving heavy artillery bombardment, followed up by the infantry seizing and defending parts of the German lines before repeating the process. The BEF commander, Lord Haig, saw it differently. He favoured an infantry breakthrough followed up by lightning cavalry advance. The result was compromise

Above *Soldiers load wounded comrades into an ambulance at Verdun.*

TIMELINE 1916

JUNE 24, 1916
Allied artillery bombardment of German lines begins during Battle of Somme.

JULY 1, 1916
British and French go over the top to the German trenches.

JULY 2-10, 1916
British fail to break through in the centre but French have some success on the right wing.

JULY 12 - AUG 27, 1916
Allied attacks and German counter-attacks.

SEPT 15-22, 1916
Battle of Flers-Courcellete; Allied attacks fail to make significant gains.

SEPT 25 - NOV 19, 1916
Battle of the Ancre sees Allies fail to break through German lines.

"That was a stupid action, because we had to make a frontal attack on bristling German guns and there was no shelter at all… There were dead bodies all over the place… We just couldn't take High Wood against machine guns. It was just absolute slaughter."

Sergeant Bill Hay, 9th Battalion, Royal Scots, 51st Division recalls an attack on 'High Wood', one of many fruitless and bloody attacks during the six months of the Somme battle.

Above *Map showing the advance of troops towards Passchendaele during the Third Battle of Ypres.*

Below Right *Lord Haig's tactics were responsible for appalling casualities during WW1.*

and confusion, with a heavy artillery barrage, but with heavy infantry attacks in the northern and central sectors.

TRAGEDY AND CONSEQUENCES

After five days of bombardment, designed to destroy German positions and shatter their barbed-wire defences, British soldiers went over the top in the early hours of July 1. Haig's plan was rigid for commanders and soldiers alike, and neither was permitted to take advantage of local circumstances. Weighed down with equipment for consolidating the enemy trenches, soldiers advanced at walking pace and

line abreast. The results were disastrous. The artillery had failed in its objectives, and German machine-gunners quickly manned their positions and slaughtered the advancing British. By nightfall 20,000 men were dead and a further 40,000 wounded – the worst day in the British army's history. Despite the mistakes, the battle continued for a further six months in a similar vein, and by its end Allied casualties had risen to more than 600,000 and German casualties to around 450,000.

STRATEGY AND AIMS

Haig's reasons for attacking the strong German defences around Ypres in Belgium continue to be a matter of fierce debate. Haig himself gave different accounts during and after the war. It is possible that he planned an advance to Ostend and Zeebrugge, to capture the German U-boat bases there. Another possibility is that he aimed to break the important rail line which supplied

"The conditions are awful, beyond description,... a desolate wilderness of water filled with shell craters,... Here a shattered wagon, there a gun mired to the muzzle in mud which grips like glue, even the birds and rats have forsaken so unnatural a spot. Mile after mile of the same unending dreariness, landmarks are gone, of whole villages hardly a pile of bricks amongst the mud marks the site. You see it best under a leaden sky with a chill drizzle falling, each hour an eternity, each dragging step a nightmare. How weirdly it recalls some half formed horror of childish nightmare.... Surely the God of Battles has deserted a spot where only devils can reign."

Major John Lyne of the 64th Brigade, Royal Field Artillery, observed the appalling conditions during the Third Battle of Ypres in 1917. The town of Passchendaele was devastated by the mortar attacks that went on around it.

the German armies, and which lay 15 km behind the Front. Alternatively, he might simply have been aiming to wear down the German forces, according to the policy of attrition that was such a feature of the strategies of both sides. Whatever his thinking, the plan and its execution had appalling consequences.

SIX BATTLES IN ONE

The Third Battle of Ypres began on July 31, 1917. Its immediate objective was to capture a strategic ridge. On the ridge lay the small town of Passchendaele that has given the battle its more popular name. Allied troops advanced over terrain churned up by artillery fire and turned into mud by rain. The Third Battle of Ypres in fact comprised six separate battles: the Battle of the Menin Road; the Battle of Polygon Wood; the Battle of Broodseinde; the Battle of Poelkapelle, and the First and Second battles of Passchendaele. Again and again, attacks were launched and failed against German defences and the weather. But Allied fighting on the Menin Road, at Polygon Wood, and at Broodseinde was successful, and on November 5, Canadian troops captured Passchendaele itself. Four months of fighting and 500,000 casualties brought no obvious Allied gain. During three days in April 1918 the Germans recaptured the ridge.

Above Soldiers advance through Chateau Wood during the Third Battle of Ypres.

Below Rows and rows of graves fill the Tynecot cemetery at Passchendaele.

TIMELINE 1917

JULY 16, 1917
British bombardment of Passchendaele.

JULY 31-AUG 18, 1917
British launch attacks in bad weather.

SEPT 20-25, 1916
Battle of the Menin Road achieves some success.

JULY 31-NOV 5
Third Battle of Ypres at Passchendaele.

"The bombardment was murderous - ours and the Germans' - and they weren't only flinging over shells, they were simply belting machine-gun fire for all they were worth… The shells were falling thick and fast and by some sort of capillary action the holes they made filled with water as you looked at them."

Private J Pickard, 7th Winnipeg Grenadiers, recalls the final push for Passchendaele.

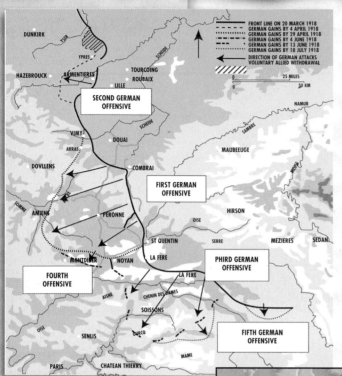

Above Map charting the failed German offensives that began in the spring of 1918.

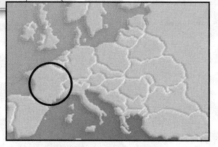

After four years of bitter conflict, the Great War came to an end on November 11 1918. Seventy million men had been mobilized, nine million had died, and millions more had been wounded. Millions of women were widowed and their children left without fathers - countless lives shattered and with an uncertain future. The shape of Europe changed for ever, the monarchies of Germany, Austro-Hungary, and Russia had been deposed, and the United States was on the brink of becoming a major world power. Reparations and war guilt were heaped on Germany, laying the foundations for a second conflict that would see mayhem and bloodshed spread across the world once more.

"We have no jealousy of German greatness, and there is nothing in this program that impairs it. We grudge her no achievement or distinction of learning or of pacific enterprise such as have made her record very bright and very enviable. We do not wish to injure her or to block in any way her legitimate influence or power."

United States President Woodrow Wilson outlined the sentiments behind US war aims in a speech given to Congress on January 8, 1918, in which he outlined what was to become known as his "Fourteen Points".

Above A US Flag drapes the Perkins building in celebration of Armistice Day, November 11, 1918.

ARMISTICE AT THE ELEVENTH HOUR

The failure of the German offensive, and the ensuing success of the Allied advance beyond the Hindenburg Line, caused morale in the German army to collapse. Though German lines were not breached, on October 3 Prince Max von Baden wrote to President Woodrow Wilson asking for a US-brokered armistice. Exactly a month later, Austro-Hungary surrendered, and on October 30, Turkey followed suit. On November 6, in a railway carriage at Compiègne, Germany signed an armistice which was to come into force at 11am on November 11, 1918. Germany agreed to withdraw from all occupied territories on the Western and Eastern fronts, and to surrender its navy. On December 1, the Allies began their occupation of the Rhineland, part of western Germany which would allow strategic control of the rest of the country. The war was over.

CELEBRATIONS AND REFLECTIONS

The victorious nations celebrated the signing of the Armistice in similar fashion. London filled with crowds of singing and cheering soldiers and civilians, and people embraced each other. In Paris, crowds sang themselves hoarse with endless renditions of the French national anthem, *la Marseillaise*. Newspapers and placards announced: 'The Armistice is signed', and patriotic crowds dragged captured German artillery around the streets. In Sydney, Australia, crowds cheered as an effigy of the Kaiser was first hanged, then burned. By contrast, Armistice Day in Germany was a sad affair. Some wept openly. The war was lost, the Kaiser had abdicated, the authoritarian Wilhelmine government was gone, and the future looked uncertain.

Above *Prince Max von Baden was charged with negotiating an armistice with the Allies.*

Right *A selection of medals awarded to British servicemen for fighting in World War 1.*

TIMELINE 1918

OCT 3, 1918
Germany asks US President Wilson to broker peace.

NOV 6, 1918
Germany signs the Armistice.

10.58 AM, NOV 11, 1918
Canadian Private George Price is one of war's last victims.

NOV 11, 1918, 11 AM
Armistice comes into force.

28 JUNE, 1919
Treaty of Versailles ends war.

15 NOV, 1920
First League of Nations meeting.

"The Kaiser and King has decided to renounce the throne. The Imperial Chancellor will remain in office until the questions connected with the abdication of the Kaiser, the renouncing by the Crown Prince of the throne of the German Empire and of Prussia, and the setting up of a regency have been settled.For the regency he intends to appoint Deputy Ebert as Imperial Chancellor, and he proposes that a bill shall be brought in for the establishment of a law providing for the immediate promulgation of general suffrage and for a constitutional German National Assembly, which will settle finally the future form of government of the German Nation and of those peoples which might be desirous of coming within the empire."

Prince Max von Baden's Announcement of Kaiser Wilhelm II's Abdication, November 9, 1918

'When the first stroke of Big Ben sounded over Whitehall, the King, standing in the middle of the road, surrounded by Admirals and Field-Marshals, turned south-wards to face the Cenotaph.

'On the last stroke of eleven, the King pressed a knob on the top of a little pedestal erected in the road, and two great Union Jacks that draped the Cenotaph fell to the ground. At the same moment the King raised his cap. Bareheaded and silent, he stood in the midst of this vast gathering of the silent people'.

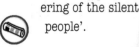

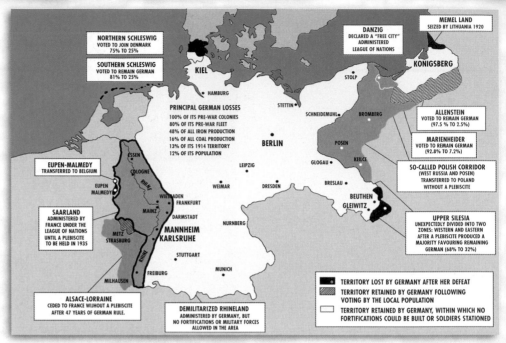

PRINCIPAL GERMAN LOSSES
100% OF ITS PRE-WAR COLONIES
80% OF ITS PRE-WAR FLEET
48% OF ALL IRON PRODUCTION
16% OF ALL COAL PRODUCTION
13% OF ITS 1914 TERRITORY
12% OF ITS POPULATION

NORTHERN SCHLESWIG
VOTED TO JOIN DENMARK
75% TO 25%

SOUTHERN SCHLESWIG
VOTED TO REMAIN GERMAN
81% TO 25%

DANZIG
DECLARED A "FREE CITY"
ADMINISTERED
LEAGUE OF NATIONS

MEMEL LAND
SEIZED BY LITHUANIA 1920

KONIGSBERG

ALLENSTEIN
VOTED TO REMAIN GERMAN
(97.5 % TO 2.5%)

MARIENHEIDER
VOTED TO REMAIN GERMAN
(92.8% TO 7.2%)

SO-CALLED POLISH CORRIDOR
(WEST RUSSIA AND POSEN)
TRANSFERRED TO POLAND
WITHOUT A PLEBISCITE

EUPEN-MALMEDY
TRANSFERRED TO BELGIUM

SAARLAND
ADMINISTERED BY FRANCE UNDER THE
LEAGUE OF NATIONS
UNTIL A PLEBISCITE
TO BE HELD IN 1935

UPPER SILESIA
UNEXPECTEDLY DIVIDED INTO TWO
ZONES: WESTERN AND EASTERN
AFTER A PLEBISCITE PRODUCED A
MAJORITY FAVOURING REMAINING
GERMAN (68% TO 32%)

ALSACE-LORRAINE
CEDED TO FRANCE WITHOUT A PLEBISCITE
AFTER 47 YEARS OF GERMAN RULE.

DEMILITARIZED RHINELAND
ADMINISTERED BY GERMANY, BUT
NO FORTIFICATIONS OR MILITARY FORCES
ALLOWED IN THE AREA

TERRITORY LOST BY GERMANY AFTER HER DEFEAT
TERRITORY RETAINED BY GERMANY FOLLOWING
VOTING BY THE LOCAL POPULATION
TERRITORY RETAINED BY GERMANY, WITHIN WHICH NO
FORTIFICATIONS COULD BE BUILT OR SOLDIERS STATIONED

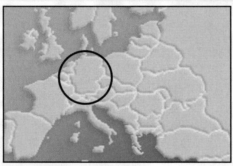

Above A map showing Germany's losses following the Treaty of Versailles.

THE TREATY OF VERSAILLES

On June 28, 1919, the leaders of the Allied forces gathered in the Hall of Mirrors at the Palace of Versailles near Paris to work out the terms of the peace settlement. Defeated Germany was not allowed to put an argument against the terms proposed and was forced to accept everything proposed. Under the Treaty Germany had to accept responsibility for starting the war; had to promise to pay reparations (compensation) of more than

'He is not missing: he is here! No words can express our feelings adequately but they will be expressed for us by the familiar bugle calls which we shall hear on the conclusion of the service'.

On July 24, 1927, the Menin Gate Memorial to the Missing at Ypres, Belgium, was inaugurated. On it are engraved the names of 55,000 soldiers whose bodies have never been identified. Field Marshal Herbert Plumer addressed the crowds and began the tradition of playing The Last Post. It is still played every day.

£6,000 million for the damage it had caused, and its army and navy were severely restricted. The German navy was restricted to just six battleships and her army a to meagre 100,000 soldiers. Added salt in the wound came in the confiscation of German territory in Europe and the loss of its colonies in Africa. Finally, the Treaty stated that Germany was not allowed to join the League of Nations, or unite with Austria.

REMEMBERING THE WAR

In the aftermath of the war the world took stock of the terrible consequences. In Europe, Britain and France put a huge effort into commemorating the sacrifices made by their people. On November 11,

Below British Prime Minister Lloyd George, French Premier Georges Clemenceau, and U.S. President Woodrow Wilson walk together in Paris during negotiations for the Treaty of Versailles.

Above Thiepval is the largest and one of the most emotive memorials to the missing from any war in which British soldiers have died. It stands in an isolated, windswept position on the Somme.

1920, the Cenotaph in London was unveiled in the presence of the King. The coffin of the Unknown Soldier, a single corpse that represented thousands, was laid to rest in Westminster Abbey. The first of many two-minute silences was observed. Across the country, in the years that followed, local war memorials were erected, as well as memorial libraries and hospitals. On July 24, 1927, the Menin Gate Memorial in Ypres, Belgium, was inaugurated in memory of 55,000 soldiers with no known grave. On July 31, 1932, the Thiepval Memorial to the 73,000 soldiers missing on the Somme battlefields was unveiled.

TIMELINE
1919-1920

1919-1939
Battlefield pilgrimages at their height.

1919
Paul Nash paints The Menin Road.

NOV 11, 1920
In London the Cenotaph is unveiled and the Unknown Soldier is buried in Westminster Abbey.

Above Flowers at the grave of the Unknown Soldier in London.

The Unknown Soldier

"Great silent crowds watched yesterday's supremely impressive tribute paid to an unknown 'common soldier'. The unveiling of the Cenotaph in Whitehall by the King, the procession thence to Westminster, and the service in the great national Abbey were of deep significance, but most impressive of all was the two minutes' of universal silence".

Daily Herald Special Correspondent, at the official unveiling of the tomb of the Unknown Soldier in Westminster Abbey, November 12, 1920.

CHAPTER 5

POPULAR CULTURE THE WAR IN THE MEDIA

Above Between 1920 and 1923, Dix painted Der Schützengraben (The Trench).

In art, literature, cinema, and photography, four years of conflict redefined the ways in which people saw themselves, each other, and their relationships with technology.

In everyday life, popular culture was saturated with the influences of war and its aftermath. New ways of seeing the world gave impetus to avant garde art such as Cubism, and new fashions such as Art Deco. Poetry, fiction, and autobiography took on a more jagged edge, while film and camera technology helped to launch the era of Hollywood.

PAINTING THE WAR

The Great War produced a dramatic shift in art. Painters found they could no longer express themselves in pre-1914 ways, and developed new and unconventional styles. In Britain, artists such as CRW Nevinson, Wyndham Lewis, and Paul Nash typified this new approach. In 1919, Nash's *The Menin Road* captured the spirit of war's devastation of the landscape. French artists produced a mix of old and new in the famous images d'Epinal. These placed the current war in a grander context of French history. The 1915 drawing *The End of the War* by Raoul Dufy is a collage that includes the Gallic symbol of a cockerel, Joan of Arc, General Joffre, and Rheims cathedral aflame after German bombardment.

In Germany, Otto Dix portrayed the grotesque nature of his war experiences. His famous painting *Flanders* mixes the nightmarish imagery of Hieronymus Bosch with the effects of industrialised war on human beings.

During the filming of **All Quiet on the Western Front,** so many (and often bizarre) cuts were made by the censors of different countries that the original uncut film has never been seen; In June 1930, for example, the film was released in Canada with the following deletions...

'dialogue in reel 3 "When you come back you'll all get some nice clean underwear" close-up of boy in hysterics in reel 4 eliminate words "in the backside" from line... "I ought to give you a kick in the backside"'

Above The Menin Road by Paul Nash. As a commissioned officer Nash produced hundreds of detailed sketches of life in the trenches on the western front, which he later developed into paintings.

PHOTOGRAPHY AND FILM

Photography and film also underwent dramatic developments during and after the war. Official war photographers took pictures for propaganda, aerial photography was perfected for planning battles, and individuals took their own personal photos. Films were of three kinds: newsreel of actual events, government-approved war films such as

Below *A still from the film* Wings *(1927), following the adventures of two fighter pilots during the war.*

Above *The powerful anti-war film* Oh What a Lovely War! *directed by Richard Attenborough.*

The Somme (1927), and Hollywood productions that presented the war in epic terms, spiced with romance and heroism. *Wings* (1927), *Hell's Angels* (1930), *Westfront* (1931) and *A Farewell to Arms* (1932) all portrayed stunning if ambiguous views of the war.

TIMELINE
1927–1930

JULY 24, 1927
Unveiling of the Menin Gate Memorial to the Missing, Ypres, Belgium.

1928
Publication of *Undertones of War*, by Edmund Blunden, *Memoirs of a Fox-Hunting Man*, by Siegfried Sassoon.

1929
Publication of *Goodbye to All That*, by Robert Graves, *The Storm of Steel*, by Ernst Jünger, *All Quiet on the Western Front*, by Erich Maria Remarque.

1930
Publication of *Memoirs of an Infantry Officer*, by Siegfried Sassoon.

"I have seen the most frightful nightmare of a country more conceived by Dante... than by nature, inspeakable, utterly indescribable. In the fifteen drawings I have made I may give you some idea of its horror... We all have a vague notion of the terrors of a battle... but no pen or drawing can convey this... Evil and the incarnate fiend alone can be master of this war and no glimmer of God's hand is seen anywhere. Sunset and sunrise are blasphemous, they are mockeries to man, only the black rain... is fit atmosphere in such a land."

Shaken by his experiences in 1917 in the Ypres Salient, Nash wrote to his wife Margaret in November 1917.

Above *A cover from the popular publication* The Illustrated War News.

Decades later, films such as Stanley Kubrick's *Paths to Glory* (1957) and Richard Attenborough's *Oh! What a Lovely War* (1969) continued to explore contentious issues raised by the Great War.

NEWSPAPERS, MAGAZINES, AND POSTERS

In a world before television or radio, news of the war came mainly from the printed media – newspapers, magazines, and posters. Propaganda fuelled much of this coverage, and the official censor deleted anything which governments regarded as too militarily sensitive or likely to reduce patriotic support for the war. Most wartime magazines were heavily illustrated with photographs and artist's impressions which often sanitised military disasters and huge casualties. In Britain

The Illustrated War News, in France *Le Miroir* and *L'Illustration*, and in Germany the *Illustrierte Zeitung*, all tailored their images and stories to suit their government's restrictions. In the battle-zones, soldiers produced their own trench newspapers such as the *British Wipers Times*, whose name was soldier's slang for Ypres.

WAR POETRY AND MEMOIRS

In war-time poetry and post-war memoirs written in English, a new language emerged to express the human experiences of war. Although

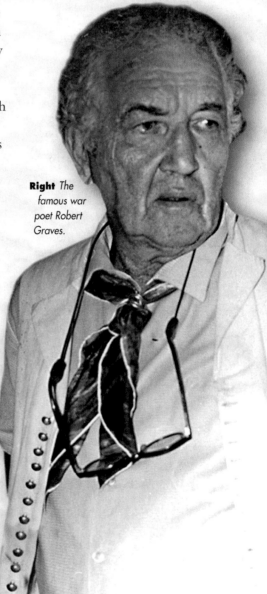

Right *The famous war poet Robert Graves.*

"One by one my contemporaries were sent out to France to take the place of casualties in the First and Second Battalions, while I remained despondently at the depôt'.

'At Béthune, I saw the ghost of a man named Private Challoner, who had been at Lancaster with me... [he] looked in at the window, saluted, and passed on. I jumped up, looked out of the window, and saw nothing except a fag-end smoking on the pavement. Challoner had been killed at Festubert in May."

Goodbye to All That by Robert Graves was published in 1931 and again with revisions in 1957; it is one of the most famous of the Great War memoirs.

written mainly by educated middle-class soldiers, poems by Wilfred Owen, Ivor Gurney, and Isaac Rosenberg captured the futility of war, and the immensity of its tragedy. A decade after 1918, many classic memoirs began to appear, often written by authors already known for writing poetry. Siegfried Sassoon published his trilogy of autobiographical war novels – *Memoirs of a Fox-Hunting Man*, *Memoirs of an Infantry Officer* and *Sherston's Progress*, Robert Graves wrote *Goodbye to All That*, and Edmund Blunden published *Undertones of War*. War poems and memoirs created and fixed the memory of the war in the public consciousness, and remain powerful evocations of the conflict today.

TRENCH ART

An important feature of the new archaeological interest in the Great War has been the study of trench art. This name describes objects made by soldiers, prisoners of war, and civilians during and after the war as souvenirs and mementoes. The most common form of trench art was created from recycled war materiel such as metal scrap and bullets, sometimes decorated with regimental badges and personalised inscriptions. The most popular item was the decorated artillery-shell case. These objects are found in museums and in people's homes as well as in excavations, and illustrate the human dimension of war.

Above In Germany, the Illustrierte Zeitung was used to portray the war from a more positive perspective.

TIMELINE 1932

JULY 31, 1932
The Memorial to the Missing at Thiepval on the Somme is unveiled.

1930
Release of the films *All Quiet on the Western Front*, *Westfront*, and *Hell's Angels*.

1932
Release of the film *A Farewell to Arms*.

Above The war poet Wilfred Owen.

*Extract from **Dulce et Decorum Est** (written in 1917 and published in 1921), one of Owen's most famous and most often quoted poems.*

"Gas! Gas! Quick, boys! - An ecstasy of fumbling,
Fitting the clumsy helmets just in time;
But someone still was yelling out and stumbling
And floundering like a man in fire or lime...

... If you could hear, at every jolt, the blood
Come gargling from the froth-corrupted lungs
Obscene as cancer, bitter as the cud
Of vile incurable sores on innocent tongues, -
My friend, you would not tell with such high zest
To children ardent for desperate glory,
The old lie: Dulce et Decorum est
Pro patria mori'."

Above *When Germany was unable to pay the reparations required, French and Belgian troops occupied the Ruhr, the centre of Germany's coal, iron and steel production.*

Below *The collapse of the German economy helped lead to the rise of the dictator Adolf Hitler.*

he Great War and its aftermath changed forever the political and economic shape of the world. It created the powerhouse of the United States, demolished imperial Europe, created new nations, fostered bitter and still-lingering ethnic tensions, and moved the world inexorably to the Second World War. Today, the war is brought to life by recorded memories, museum exhibitions, books, television and film. Since the 1960s, there has been a huge surge of interest in the war which has led to the development of tourism to the Western Front battlefields.

TOWARDS A NEW WAR

The First World War ended officially with the Treaty of Versailles on June 28, 1919. However, as many foresaw at the time, the terms were so harsh for Germany that they would breed only resentment and political extremism. The 'war to end all wars' became instead a twenty-year-long lead-in to the outbreak of the Second World War in 1939. The aftermath of the Versailles Treaty during the inter-war years changed the shape of the world. Despite the fact that the Versailles Treaty had embodied some of President Woodrow Wilson's Fourteen Points for World Peace, the United States Senate refused to ratify the

"The treaty includes no provisions for the economic rehabilitation of Europe—nothing to make the defeated Central empires into good neighbors, nothing to stabilize the new states of Europe, nothing to reclaim Russia; nor does it promote in any way a compact of economic solidarity amongst the Allies themselves; no arrangement was reached at Paris for restoring the disordered finances of France and Italy, or to adjust the systems of the Old World and the New."

Excerpts from The Economic Consequences of the Peace by John Maynard Keynes, published in 1920.

Treaty of Versailles. Precisely when American leadership was required, the country slid further into an isolationist policy, which precluded any help with global financial restructuring, and debt repayment. In Germany, many believed that their Army had not been defeated, and that incompetent politicians and communist agitators had caused a collapse from within. German humiliation was exacerbated when French troops occupied the industrial region of the Ruhr in 1921 when Germany defaulted on repayment. The Versailles Treaty had stipulated that Germany could only keep 100,000 men under arms. So many ex-soldiers joined far-right extremist groups during the social and economic chaos of the 1920s. These developments, combined with rampant inflation and the German government's inability to deal with it culminated in the formation of the National Socialist (Nazi) Party under the leadership of Adolf Hitler, appointed Chancellor in 1933.

A NEW EUROPE

In Europe, also, the inter-war period saw ominous political developments. Italy felt she had been shabbily treated

Above In Italy, the fascist dictator Benito Mussolini rose to power on the back of national unrest, a consequence of the harsh terms set down at the Treaty of Versailles.

at Versailles despite being on the Allied side. This gave the opportunity to Benito Mussolini and his followers, the fascisti, to seize political power. The political map of eastern Europe was also redrawn during this period, with Finland, Czechoslovakia, Poland, and Yugoslavia all coming into being after 1919. Many of these new states were weak, however, and did little other than create a bitterly divisive legacy for

TIMELINE 1939-1964

1939-1964
Interest in the First World War reaches its lowest ebb.

1964
Broadcast of BBC's *The Great War* stimulates renewed interest in the First World War.

Battlefield tourism to the Western Front becomes a major commercial phenomenon.

Below Despite Woodrow Wilson's role in formulating the Treaty of Versailles, after World War 1 the United States became more isolationist.

"National aspirations must be respected; people may now be dominated and governed only by their own consent. "Self determination" is not a mere phrase. It is an imperative principle of action, which statesmen will henceforth ignore at their peril. This war had its roots in the disregard of the rights of small nations and of nationalities which lacked the union and the force to make good their claim to determine their own allegiances and their own forms of political life. Covenants must now be entered into which will render such things impossible for the future; and those covenants must be backed by the united force of all nations that love justice and are willing to maintain it at any cost..."

Excerpt from speech to Congress by Woodrow Wilson, Feb 11, 1919

Above *Four American representatives arrive at the conference at Lausannes in 1922 to decide the future of the Ottoman Empire. From left to right are Mr. Berlin, Secretary-General: Ambassador Child, American representative at Rome; Mr. Lorio, U.S. Minister at Bern, and Mr. Armory, Secretary of the American delegation.*

Dear James,

Whilst perhaps enjoyment is the wrong word to use we did enjoy your excellent guiding. We are both glad we went and somehow I feel it was something that as many people as possible should try and do in order to understand better the horrors of War. I will never forget the emotion of standing under the Thiepval Memorial and trying to comprehend the massive scale of killing that took place and what little was achieved, but I suppose we can all claim the knowledge of hindsight.

A letter of thanks written to Somme Battlefield Tours Limited, a European company offering guided tours of World War 1 battlefields.

the future. This legacy continued through the Second World War, the Cold War, the collapse of the Soviet empire during the 1980s, and eventually contributed to the bitter struggles in Bosnia-Herzegovina and Kosovo during the 1990s.

PROBLEMS IN THE MIDDLE EAST

The Middle East also suffered the consequences of the Versailles Treaty in ways which were to have a profound impact up to the present day. Arab lands freed when Germany's ally the Ottoman Empire surrendered were not given their independence at Versailles. Vast areas were arbitrarily divided up and territorial boundaries drawn, with

the resultant new nations given as mandates to the British and French to administer. These actions sowed the seeds of many current problems in the region associated with nationalism, religion, and the control of oil production.

BATTLEFIELD TOURISM

During the inter-war years, tens of thousands of pilgrims and tourists visited the battlefields of the old Western Front. Clutching old letters, maps, and guidebooks, they journeyed on coaches to the Somme and Ypres, stopping briefly at the sites and towns associated with four years of war. They stayed in local hostels, ate and drank in cafés and bars, and bought poignant battlefield souvenirs to take home. Battlefield tourism helped rebuild the shattered local economies. The Second World War brought battlefield pilgrimages to an abrupt end. But the arrival of television stimulated the desire of many to visit the Western Front's battlefields, and during the early 1970s there were 50,000 visitors a year. By 1974, this had grown to 250,000 a year. Personal enquiries to the Commonwealth War Graves Commission (CWGC) concerning the whereabouts of graves rose from 1500 a year in the mid-1960s to 28,000 in 1990. Today, numbers continue to grow rapidly, and are catered for by an ever-increasing number of hotels, cafés, and battlefield tour companies. The 'Last Post' ceremony in Ypres takes place every evening at 8pm and attracts large numbers of visitors.

Left *Battlefield tourists view a reconstructed trench in the Somme.*

Above *Bugles are played during the Last Post at Ypres.*

TIMELINE 1990– 1998

1990
Digging begins, mainly by local amateur groups; several professional rescue excavations in France.
Battlefield reclamation and scavenging goes on.

1992
The Historial de la Grande Guerre opens in Peronne on the Somme in France.

1997
Professional excavations begin at Auchonvillers on the Somme; investigations of trench art begin.

1998
The *In Flanders Fields* Museum opens in Ypres, Belgium.

MUSEUMS, MONUMENTS, AND HERITAGE

Beginning in the 1960s, and gaining momentum during the 1990s, the First World War changed from a specialist interest to an iconic cultural event. It became a potent mix of rejuvenated battlefield tourism, incorporating beautifully-kept war cemeteries, war museums and exhibitions, and older and newly-built memorials. The idea of the war as heritage had arrived. In Britain the Imperial War Museum organizes major exhibitions, a National Inventory of War Memorials has been established, and the two-minute silence on November 11 is observed by increasing numbers of people.

Above *The imposing front of the Imperial War Museum in London.*

"The United States Congress created the Veterans History Project in 2000. It collects oral history interviews, memoirs, letters, diaries, photographs, and other original materials from veterans of World Wars I and II, and the Korean, Vietnam, and Persian Gulf Wars and the Afghanistan and Iraq conflicts (2001-present). Those US citizen civilians who were actively involved in supporting war efforts (such as war industry workers, USO workers, flight instructors, medical volunteers, etc.) are also encouraged to contribute their personal narratives. Members of the public become part of the Veterans History Project after they donate their materials."

Official statement plan from the Library of Congress Veterans History Project.

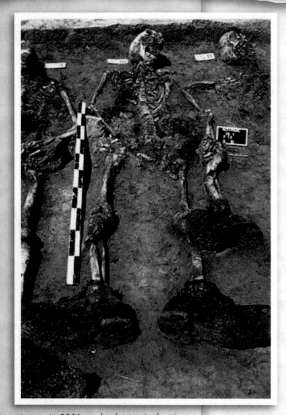

Above In 2001, archeologists in the city of Arras, northern France discovered the remains of 24 British servicemen who were buried in 1917 during World War I. They were unearthed during the excavations for a new BMW car plant.

In France and Belgium, the 'Western Front Experience' has become commercialised. Tourist boards in Ypres and on the Somme organize special events, and local hotels, restaurants, and shops associate themselves with Great War imagery.

BATTLEFIELD ARCHAEOLOGY

It is only recently that the First World War has been seen as worth studying archaeologically. In 2001, a mass grave of twelve German soldiers was uncovered at Gavrelle, revealing skeletons, still wearing helmets, and apparently hastily buried by their comrades. In Belgian Flanders, in the old Ypres Salient battlefield, local amateur groups carried out excavations until 2002. Then, the Belgian Institute for the Archaeological Heritage of Western Flanders became officially involved. Its first investigation was an excavation in the path of the A19 motorway extension outside Ypres. Archaeological reconnaissance included aerial photographs, trench maps, and contemporary accounts of the fighting, as well as interviewing local residents and field-walking. This comprehensive approach identified nine zones for investigation. They revealed differences between German and British structures, seven human bodies, trench systems, duckboards, ammunition and soldiers' equipment. Since 2002, professional archaeology has arrived on the battlefields of the Western Front. The most important development was the establishment in 2002 of the first Department of First World War Archaeology in Belgium, which focused attention on who should be allowed to excavate, how, where, and when?

"Remains unearthed from the fields of Passchendaele provide a timely reminder of the brutality of trench life."

Yesterday, a few miles north of Ypres, the remains of another nameless British soldier were being unearthed. Not much was left - a few bones, some buttons and a pair of boots - lying in the crater gouged by the shell that killed him. Over the last few months, a team of British and Belgian archaeologists have been busy excavating a trench system near the village of St Jan. The site is on the route of a new motorway and the government in Brussels decreed that it should be thoroughly researched. Six British dead have been recovered and, for once, a name may soon be attached to one of them. William Storey was barely a man when he signed up for the Northumberland Fusiliers. From Blyth, Northumberland, he was part of a detachment from the regiment's 5th Battalion, which went into action on Oct 26, 1917. In all probability he was killed by a shell while waiting to go forward.

Daily Telegraph report, 11th Nov, 2003.

PROTECTING MEMORIES

The excavation of First World War sites involves recent events which are still just within living memory. This makes investigations sensitive and difficult for those who dig and visit. Media coverage often highlights images of the skeletons of unknown soldiers, emphasizing that these could be our grandfathers or great-uncles. This is made more emotional and personal because of the hundreds of thousands of unidentified bodies still lying on the battlefields. Their names are engraved on huge war memorials to 'The Missing' at Thiepval on the Somme, and at Tynecot and the Menin Gate in Belgian Flanders. The American Battle Monuments Commission, set up by an act of Congress in 1923, honours the sacrifices of US war dead. In the US, November 11 is known as Veterans' Day, and is marked by services at various memorials.

Below Items recovered from the battlefields of Flanders by the Institute for the Archaeological Heritage of Western Flanders.

Above *Belgian archaeologists excavate a serpentine trench at Crossroads Farm, the infamous no man's land between the warring forces.*

Below *An aerial photograph taken in no man's land reveals clearly visible trenches.*

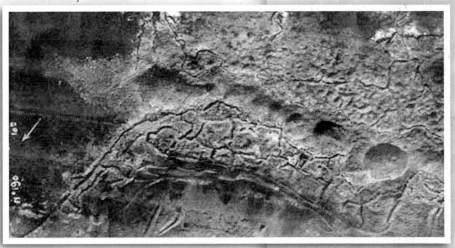

TIMELINE 2002-2004

2002
Establishment of the Department of First World War archaeology in Belgian Flanders.

2004
Professional excavations at Serre, Somme.

"Flanders still yields remains
Shoe and bones of unidentified WWI soldier unearthed in Ypres, Belgium."

Eighty-five years after the end of World War I, investigators are still finding remains of soldiers who perished in Flanders fields -- site of some of the war's most intense fighting. They uncovered the remains of a British soldier Friday, the seventh serviceman found since excavations began a year ago on Pilkem Ridge, where 12,000 men died in one day in 1917 at the start of the third Battle of Ypres. In the surrounding area of southwest Belgium, remains belonging to dozens of soldiers are found every year, mostly by farmers at plowing time. "They call it the harvest of bones," said Peter Francis of the Commonwealth War Graves Commission, in Maidenhead, England. German and Allied armies fought in Flanders for over four years in some of the war's most intensive trench warfare. The slaughter was memorialized in an anguished poem by Canadian army surgeon John McCrae:
"In Flanders fields the poppies blow between the crosses, row on row... "

CNN Report, Tuesday, November 11, 2003

Two important aspects of the war's major figures were the old age of the generals who fought the battles, and the variable quality of the politicians who directed it. On all sides, generals and politicians were caught in the same dilemma - how to fight a modern industrialised total war with ideas, strategies, and tactics that were either untested, or had been inherited from quite different nineteenth-century wars. Attitudes towards new war technologies such as the machine gun, aeroplanes, gas, and massed artillery barrage were either contemptuous or ill-thought-out, and untold millions of men died or were mutilated as a result.

KAISER WILHELM II (1859-1941)

Trained in the Prussian Army tradition, Wilhelm II became German Kaiser in 1888. He believed passionately that Germany should become a world power to rival Britain, and supported the building up of the Army and Navy. He dismissed the Iron Chancellor Otto von Bismarck in 1890 and appointed his own generals during the war. As the personification of a militarised imperial Germany he was forced to abdicate when his army faltered in 1918 and the Armistice was signed. He moved to Doorn in Holland where he lived the rest of his life.

DAVID LLOYD GEORGE (1863-1945)

Famous for his oratory, Lloyd George entered politics as a Liberal MP in 1890. From 1908 until 1914 he was Chancellor of the Exchequer, and became Minister of Munitions in 1915. He served as Prime Minister between 1916–18, during which time he tried in vain to take war policy away from the military. He was particularly critical of Haig's conduct of the battles of the Somme and Passchendaele. Aggressively pro-war, he served a second term as prime minister from 1918 until 1922.

CZAR NICHOLAS II

Czar of all the Russias in 1914, Nicholas II was the autocratic ruler of a sprawling multinational empire of 150 million people. Shy and unworldly, he ruled over an almost medieval rural society which was unprepared for the outbreak of industrialised war. He failed to inspire leadership or to make crucial political changes. In 1917, civil unrest developed into the Russian Revolution and the Czar and his family were murdered a year later.

THOMAS WOODROW WILSON (1856-1924)

Thomas Woodrow Wilson was born on December 28, 1856. He was an American scholar who was passionate about literature and politics and decided to pursue a career in the latter. Wilson was elected Democratic Governor of New York in 1910, and US President in 1912. Re-elected four years later in the middle of the war, he tried in vain to keep the United States neutral. Provoked by German intrigues with Mexico and unrestricted submarine warfare, Wilson declared for the Allies in April 1917, and began mobilising the US Army under General Pershing. He was centre-stage after the war, negotiating successfully for the creation of the League of Nations. Despite this he lost the 1920 election by a landslide margin.

LORD KITCHENER OF KHARTOUM (1850-1916)

Kitchener was 64 in 1914 when he became British Secretary of State for War. He began his army career in the Royal Engineers, and rose to prominence in Britain's many colonial conflicts in Africa, including a role in successfully repelling anti-colonialist forces in Sudan after which he was made a Lord. His most important contribution was to recognise the need for a large volunteer force to reinforce the small professional army of the time. The so-called Kitchener Armies were recruited with the aid of the famous 'Your Country Needs You!' poster showing his face and a pointing finger. Millions responded to the call. He died unexpectedly in 1916 en route to Russia when his ship HMS *Hampshire* was hit by a mine in the Baltic.

GENERAL PAUL VON HINDENBURG (1847-1934)

Hindenburg was 66 years old in 1914 and was brought out of retirement to successfully command the German Eighth Army on the Eastern Front between 1914-16. Hero status followed and he was appointed chief-of-staff in 1916, ending the slaughter at Verdun and building the defensive Hindenburg Line. The failure of his Spring 1918 offensive led to the Armistice of November 11. Despite this defeat, Hindenburg became president of the Weimar Republic in 1925. Hindenburg is well known for his fateful decision to appoint the Nazi leader Adolf Hitler as Chancellor in 1933, a decision that would ultimately propel the world into another global conflict. Hindenburg died in 1934.

DOUGLAS, FIRST EARL HAIG (Field Marshal Lord) Haig

Haig is arguably the most controversial British military figure of the war. He was the classic example of a professional cavalry officer whose ideas and tactics belonged to small-scale 19th-century colonial conflicts. Before World War 1, Haig served in India, South Africa and the Sudan, and was eventually appointed director of military training at the War Office in 1906. Despite this record, Haig was slow to adapt to the dramatically changed circumstances of industrialised war fought by trench-bound infantry. One consequence was the terrible loss of British soldiers during the battles of the Somme (1916) and Passchendaele (1917). He persevered and learned from his mistakes, taking his forces to final victory in 1918.

GENERAL JOSEPH JACQUES JOFFRE (1852-1931)

Joseph Joffre was of humble origin, but rose to become the dominant French figure in World War 1 until 1916. He served in the Franco-Prussian war in 1870-1871, as well as in several colonial campaigns, and also worked as a military engineer; By the time World War I broke out, Joffre was 63 years old yet he became commander-in-chief of the French Army during this momentous period of history. General Joffre successfully stopped the German advance at the First Battle of the Marne in September 1914. He then played a less active role in the war, and in 1916 after the Battle of Verdun he was removed from office.

GENERAL HENRI PHILIPPE PÉTAIN (1856-1951)

Compared to other generals of the time, Henri Phillippe Pétain was cautious in his tactics and advocated the strategy of strong defence rather than endless and costly infantry attacks. He put this into practice at Verdun in 1916. In 1917 at the age of 61, he was appointed Commander-in-Chief of the French Army, replacing General Nivelle. Pétain became a controversial figure during the Second World War, governing Nazi-occupied France under the Vichy regime for the Germans. During this time he was implicated in the deportation of many French Jews to their deaths. Although sentenced to death in 1945, Charles de Gaulle commuted the sentence.

GENERAL ERICH VON FALKENHAYN (1861-1922)

Falkenhayn rose to prominence as a member of the International force during the Boxer Rebellion in China in 1900. In 1913, Falkenhayn was Prussian Minister of War. After the Schlieffen Plan had failed to deliver a quick victory he revitalised Germany's military strategy, devising the idea of attrition to wear down the Allied armies. Convinced that the Western Front was the key battle-zone, he put his policies into practice at Verdun in 1916. The terrible losses suffered by the German Army for only a limited success led to his being replaced by Hindenburg and Ludendorff. Falkenhayn was transferred to the Transylvanian Front, where he had success in defeating Romanian forces. Falkenhayn died in 1922.

GENERAL ERICH VON LUDENDORFF (1856-1937)

In 1914, von Ludendorff was Quartermaster General of the German Second Army. His qualities as a tactician led to the successful invasion of Belgium and particularly the capture of Liège. As Chief-of-Staff to Hindenburg he mobilised Germany for total war, and initiated the controversial policy of submarine warfare which convinced the United States to enter the war. After the German defeat, von Ludendorff moved to Sweden where he took up a career as a writer, lauding the abilities of the vanquished German forces. von Ludendorff returned to Germany in the 1920s, where he took part in Hitler's failed Nazi rising in Munich. Despite this, he continued to represent the Nazis, and stood in the Reichstag from 1924–1928. He died in 1937, and among the mourners was Adolf Hitler.

MARSHAL FERDINAND FOCH (1851-1929)

Ferdinand Foch served in the Franco-Prussian War, and developed a reputation for expertise in artillery tactics. Foch played a crucial role in achieving French success at the First Battle of the Marne in 1914. His greatest achievement however lay in becoming the first Commander-in-Chief of all Allied Armies in March 1918. With the strong-willed generals Haig, Pétain, and Pershing under his authority, Foch devised and carried to success a true grand strategy which led to German capitulation in November 1918. He was greatly praised and decorated by the victorious nations after the war. Foch warned that the harsh terms of Versailles would lead to future trouble. He died in 1929.

GLOSSARY

Allies British Empire, France, Russia, Belgium, Serbia, Italy, Japan, China, and USA.

ANZAC Acronym applied to the armed forces of Australia and New Zealand.

Armistice The agreement to suspend hostilities on November 11, 1918.

Attrition Strategy employed by both sides involving the wearing down of enemy resources of men and materiel by continuous attacks, as at Verdun in 1916.

Battalion Unit of infantry in the British army, comprising three or four companies and about 1,000 men.

Billet Accommodation for military personnel when not fighting - usually in requisitioned civilian houses.

'Bite and hold' Strategy involving attacking, winning and then consolidating the enemy's trenches which provokes costly counter-attacks.

Brigade Unit of a British Army division, comprising four to six battalions.

British Expeditionary Force (BEF) Term originally given to the six British divisions sent to France in 1914 and later to all the armies of the British Empire serving in France.

Casualty Clearing Station Medical station near to the front line giving immediate treatment to soldiers.

Central Powers German Empire, Austro-Hungarian Empire, Turkey, and Bulgaria.

Communication trench Trench connecting the front-line with the support-line trenches.

Company Unit of British infantry battalion; between 150-250 men.

Conscript Men who were forced by law to serve in the armed forces.

Court martial Military court which tried and sentenced soldiers who had broken military (martial) law.

Demilitarization The removal or reduction of military forces from an area or country.

Demobilization The dismantling of army units and the return of soldiers to civilian life.

Dugout Underground shelter in the trenches used by soldiers of all armies for protection against bombardment and attack.

Entente French term describing the alliance between the United Kingdom, France, and Russia.

Freikorps German paramilitary units composed of ex-army men.

General Headquarters (GHQ) The office of the British Army's commander-in-chief.

Genocide Systematic extermination of racial groups.

Hindenburg Line Defensive line of barbed wire, trenches, and fortifications built by the Germans and to which they withdrew in 1917.

Hindenburg Plan A plan to place the German economy and armaments production under military control.

Home Front The civilian war effort at home.

Indemnity Payment made by the defeated country as compensation for damage inflicted by war.

League of Nations International organization of sovereign countries set up during the interwar years to keep the peace and settle disputes through negotiation. The precursor of the United Nations.

Logistics Support system of materiel and services given to armies to keep them effective as fighting forces.

Marianne Female figure representing the personification of France and her people.

Materiel Equipment used by the military.

mobilization process of calling up the reserves of the armed forces to maximize military strength.

Munitions Mainly refers to artillery shells and rifle and machine-gun bullets.

Munitionettes Name given to women who replaced men in the munitions factories.

No man's land The dangerous open space between two opposing trench lines.

Noncombatant Individual whose wartime duties excluded fighting.

Pals' Battalions British battalions composed of men recruited from a single location, either a town or workplace.

Poilu French term meaning 'hairy' applied to the French Army's infantrymen.

Pioneer Company Units of soldiers who dug trenches and engaged in labouring works behind the front lines.

Propaganda Selective broadcast of information designed to influence public opinion.

Reichstag The elected legislative body of Germany.

Reparations Payments of money and materials made by the defeated countries to the victors after 1918.

Salient Name given to an area where one side's forces projected beyond their own front-line into that of the enemy's lines, as in the famous Ypres Salient in Belgium.

Schlieffen Plan Military plan named after the German Count Alfred von Schlieffen designed to enable Germany to fight on two fronts by quickly knocking France out of the war.

Shrapnel Artillery-shell fragments designed to kill and maim.

Soviet Elected councils of workers and soldiers in Russia in 1917.

Spanish Flu The outbreak of influenza between 1918-19 which killed more people than the war itself.

'Stand To' The British Army's order to adopt firing positions against the enemy.

Strategy Overall plan for the large-scale conduct of war.

Tactics Small-scale conduct of war.

Tirpitz Plan Plan devised by Admiral Tirpitz to make Germany into a major naval power and so a rival to the United Kingdom's Royal Navy.

Tommy Atkins Nickname given to British infantrymen.

Total War The militarization of a country's economy and its dedication to the war effort.

Treaty of Versailles Peace treaty signed on 28 June 1919 which brought the First World War to an official end.

Trench Art Term given to objects made by soldiers and civilians usually of recycled war scrap and intended as souvenirs for sale.

Weimar Republic The democratic government of Germany after 1918 which took its name from the town of Weimar where it was originally based.

White Russians Armed forces of Russians and Allies who opposed the Bolshevik government.

INDEX

ACKNOWLEDGEMENTS

PICTURE CREDITS:

Every effort has been made to trace the copyright holders, and we apologize in advance for any unintentional omissions. We would be pleased to insert the appropriate acknowledgements in any subsequent edition of this publication.

B=bottom; C=centre; L=left; R=right; T=top

Alamy: 22b, 23t. Art Archive: 5tr, 6b,17br, 30 all, 32t, 33t. Corbis: 5br, 6-7b, 7b, 8t,11t, 16c, 17c, 24c, 25b, 28–29b, 38–39 all. Everett Collection: 31 all. Getty Images: 12c, 13r. Imperial War Museum: 10–11b. Mary Evans Picture Library: 8-9c, 10t, 10cl.

QED
Word Banks

Copyright © QED Publishing 2005

First published in the UK in 2005 by
QED Publishing
A Quarto Group company
226 City Road
London EC1V 2TT
www.qed-publishing.co.uk

A Catalogue record for this book is available from the British Library.

ISBN 1 84538 458 X

Written by Wendy Body
Designed by Alix Wood
Editor Hannah Ray
Illustrated by Sanja Rescek

Series Consultant Anne Faundez
Publisher Steve Evans
Creative Director Louise Morley
Editorial Manager Jean Coppendale

Printed and bound in China

Word Banks

MUP'S

Days of the Week

Wendy Body

QED Publishing

On **Monday**, Mup climbed a mountain with a rainbow in his pocket.

4

Monday

Tuesday

Wednesday

Thursday

Friday

Saturday

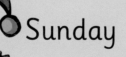 Sunday

On **Tuesday**, he flew to the
moon and back in a shiny,
silver rocket.

Monday

Tuesday

Wednesday

Thursday

Friday

Saturday

Sunday

On **Wednesday**, he walked to the North Pole and played with a polar bear.

Monday

Tuesday

Wednesday

Thursday

Friday

Saturday

Sunday

On **Thursday**, he made an enormous cake for all his friends to share.

10

Monday

Tuesday

Wednesday

Thursday

Friday

Saturday

Sunday

On **Friday**, he had a ride on a whale and went sailing all over the sea.

Monday

Tuesday

Wednesday

Thursday

Friday

Saturday

Sunday

On **Saturday**, he
built a castle at the
top of a very tall tree.

14

Monday

Tuesday

Wednesday

Thursday

Friday

Saturday

Sunday

On **Sunday**, he went in
a hot-air balloon to fly all
over the sky, and painted
the clouds with purple
paint when they came
drifting by.

16

Monday

Tuesday

Wednesday

Thursday

Friday

Saturday

Sunday

Mup's Diary

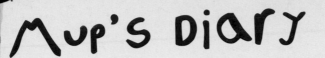

Monday

climbed a mountain

Tuesday

flew to the moon

Wednesday

walked to the North Pole

Thursday
made an enormous cake

Friday
sailed on a whale

Saturday

built a castle

Sunday

painted the clouds

Things to do

Can you complete the sentences by pointing to the right day of the week?

Monday
Saturday
Wednesday
Friday
Thursday
Sunday
Tuesday

On _____ Mup climbed a mountain.

On _____ Mup flew to the moon.

On _____ Mup walked to the North Pole.

On _____ Mup made an enormous cake.

On _____ Mup went on a whale.

On _____ Mup built a castle.

On _____ Mup painted the clouds.

Things to do

Can you remember how the words for these pictures begin?

Which words begin with the same sound?

Word bank

Words from the story

balloon
bear
cake
castle
cloud
moon
mountain
pocket
rainbow
rocket
sea
tree
whale

Action words

built
climbed
flew
painted
played
walked

Word bank

Words and endings

build	built	
climb	climbed	
fly	flew	
paint	painted	
play	played	
walk	walked	

What do you notice
about these words?

More action words

draw
hop
jump
run
skip
sit
swim
stand

Parents' and teachers' notes

- As you read the book to your child, run your finger along underneath the text. This will help your child to follow the reading and focus on the look of the words, as well as their sound.

- Once your child is familiar with the book, encourage him or her to join in with the reading – especially the days of the week.

- Help your child to both see and understand the illustrations. Use open-ended questions to encourage him or her to respond, e.g. 'What's happening on this page?' 'What is Mup doing here?' 'Could he really do that?'

- Practise saying the days of the week in order.

- Can your child remember what Mup did on particular days?

- Encourage your child to express opinions and preferences. Ask questions such as, 'Which picture do you like most? Why?' 'Which part of the book did you like best?' 'Which day do you think Mup enjoyed most?' 'If you could do any of the things that Mup did, which would you choose? Why?'

- Ask your child to make comparisons between Mup and himself or herself, e.g. 'Today is Monday (for example). What did Mup do yesterday? What did you do yesterday?' Discuss what your child might do over the course of a week. Are there certain things he or she does on particular days?

- Talk about Mup and discuss the monster's appearance. Encourage your child to invent and describe a monster of his or her own. What things would the monster like to do? What might feature in the monster's diary?

- Draw your child's attention to the structure of some words – especially the days of the week. Look at how each one includes the smaller word 'day'. Explain that this can help us to remember how the words are spelled, e.g. 'Wednesday' is spelled 'Wed–nes–day'.

- Read the instructions/questions on the 'Things to do' pages (pages 20–21) to your child and help him or her with the answers where necessary. Give your child lots of encouragement and praise. Even if he or she gets something wrong you can say: 'That was a really good try but it's not that one it's this one.'

- Read and discuss the words on the 'Word bank' pages (pages 22–23). Look at the letter patterns together and how the words are spelled. Cover up the first part of a word and see if your child can remember what was there. See if your child can write the simpler words from memory – he or she is likely to need several attempts to write a word correctly!

- When you are talking about letter sounds, try not to add too much of an uh or er sound. Say mmm instead of muh or mer, ssss instead of suh or ser. Saying letter sounds as carefully as possible will help your child when he or she is trying to build up or spell words – ter-o-per doesn't sound much like 'top'!

- Talk about words: what they mean, how they sound, how they look and how they are spelled; but if your child gets restless or bored, stop. Enjoyment of the story, activity or book is essential if we want children to grow up valuing books and reading!